ISBN 979-8-9913942-1-5

Published by Hidden Hand Press
www.hiddenhandbooks.com

HIDDEN HAND PRESS

Death
Is
A
Tease

Brianna Malotke

CONTENTS

FOREWORD

PREFACE

I: FULL OF RAGE

II: WHAT IS LOVE?

III: Confessing to Death

ABOUT THE AUTHOR

Brianna Malotke has snagged the moments in life that strip us bare, leaving only the rawness of our emotions—rage, love, grief, and the fragile hope for something better. Her words linger in those spaces we often try to avoid, asking us to pause, breathe, and take stock of what it means to truly feel. These poems are an invitation to sit with those feelings, to acknowledge the scars they leave behind, and to find strength in their honesty. With delicate precision and unflinching courage, Brianna has captured the essence of human vulnerability and resilience in a way that feels deeply personal yet universally relatable.

Each section of this collection guides us through a different stage of reckoning with life's complexities. From the fiery anger that demands to be felt, to the tender moments of love that heal our wounds, and finally, to the quiet conversations we have with grief and mortality—every poem holds a mirror to our shared humanity. Brianna's work transcends mere reflection; it speaks to the raw truths of our existence, gently coaxing us to embrace every messy, beautiful facet of it.

These words are more than poetry—they are a safe space for those who have loved deeply, lost painfully, and still found the courage to continue. In each stanza, Brianna reminds us that the act of feeling, even when it hurts, is a testament to our strength. This work offers not only solace but also hope, reminding us that even in our darkest moments, there is beauty in feeling, in enduring, and in becoming whole again.

Here is an opportunity to remember what it means to be fully human.

Angela Yuriko Smith
November 21, 2024
Rio do Sul, Brasil

Dealing with love and loss – whether it's a successful relationship, trying to heal your inner self, or grieving for someone who's gone – this poetry collection dives into intense emotions that people experience as they try to find a place for themselves.

This poetry collection is full of intense emotions that are portrayed with some actions that warrant trigger warnings. These TW include: mental illness, self-harm, suicide, and discussions of death.

PART I :

FULL OF RAGE

STAND TALL

No longer flinching, fists curl
In response, run away,

Far away, until the voice
Inside my head declares
That I'm finally safe, free.

Yet the anger still grows
Inside me no matter
The distance between us.

Why do I need to be the bigger person?

Fists clenched until I bleed.
Time may heal wounds, but I'll
Never forget your actions.

Rage is a part of me now.

CAN'T CHANGE

The memories haunt my dreams.
Unable to let go, I cling to her
Tightly, until my palms ache.

And then I wake.

She remains there, trapped.
Looking out the window, yearning
To feel the night air against her skin.

The dewy grass beneath her feet as she flees.

Her and I, we come from a broken place
Where everything is twisted and ugly
And thick skin still bleeds.

And the day continues, and my anger

Lurks around the corner, too active

For cobwebs to settle in.

Can't change what you've done.

Can I Scream Now?

The words linger,
Cowering at the back
Of my throat.

My inner child screaming
As the pain brings memories
Bubbling to the surface.

I shake her, begging her
To stop the noise, fearful
For all she's released.

The words on the tip
Of my tongue—maybe
I too can scream now.

I hold her hand, this
Piece of me I shielded,
I tried to protect.

The words are not quite

Right, but they are the truth—

We will heal together.

MADE OF GLASS

Anger lingers on my skin.
Inhuman in feeling, this rage
Cuts and bruises me.
Somehow still standing, waiting
For cracks that never heal.

It's okay, a fleeting whisper.

I'm glass, the grief much
Too heavy—I crack beneath
The weight of it all.

No one to protect me.
Too young to be alone
Against the pain that ails me.

You'll be okay, a fleeting whisper.
Alone in a void, my screams silent
As the tears fall—alone, just a child.

ONE DAY

Sometimes I want to scream
But nothing comes out —the silence
A burden I continue to bear alone.

My muscles ache and my joints stiffen
From holding my tongue and clenching
My jaw—holding it all inside.

Sometimes I want to scream
But I'll never feel that catharsis.
Bound by silence and grief,
They hold both my hands.

Perhaps one day I'll let go.

LIKE LIGHTNING

My head's been in hell.
With a dagger
I'll cut every piece
Of you from myself.

Like lightning,
I won't let you
Strike twice.

Shatter my ribs from
Hugging myself
Too tight, trying to heal.

Memories haunt me
Like a ghost lingering
Inside a home.

The fury festers deep
Down inside.

How can I ever gloss

Over my childhood?

Left Behind

Parts of me died the day
You raised your voice.

Sometimes, I visit her
In my dreams—the fragment
Of myself left behind.

The nightmares encroach;
Yet, she remains still.

Parts of me died each time
You raised your voice.

Sometimes, I think she's
Healed and whole, but
There are pieces missing.

Never smiling, she waits
For the silence we craved.

Parts of me are full of rage

And others long to forget.

KITCHEN THOUGHTS

Until my throat is dry, scratched
And hoarse I scream—my voice
Nothing more than a squeak.

Yet I still cry out, pleading
For your attention but you look away.
Tears fall, for we both know
The apology, I desperately
Seek will never leave your lungs.
It might be nestled deep, deep down
Inside, but it'll never grace my ears.

And in another universe, I'm just a child,
Sitting at the kitchen table, surrounded
By love, and fear never crosses the threshold.

And you tell me you love me,
That you're proud, but I'm just child,
Just a teenager, a daughter.

And still I cry; in another universe

You're never a parent

And you live a full life.

No regrets sitting in your kitchen.

Destined for Rage

How much of our parents
Are we destined to become?

Do you feel it when you
Raise your voice?

The fear turning to rage?

Do you feel it when you
Curse the fates?

For molding into what you
Said you'd never become.

READY TO ASK

I need help—the words reverberate.

Against my ribs—the screams made my throat hoarse.

I need help—and I'm ready to ask.

I clawed my way back from the grave that

I dug for myself, the blood on my hands

Dry and cracked, dirt all over my limbs.

I need help—and I called my mother.

But when she answered, I turned into

That ten-year-old girl sitting at the

Kitchen table too young – independent

For her age they claim – to be alone.

Yet she sat there, as I do now

Knowing the words I want to say

Will never make their way to you

I needed help and all we discussed was gardening.

Stealing Sunlight

Born with tragedy
Pumping through their veins,
Sadness-tinged blood.

Let the anger grow,
Like vines around a tree,
Weaving themselves
Suffocating everything.

Survival, that's all that is left.

AN OUNCE STRONGER

A begging to be believed—

I grew much too tired,
Not an ounce stronger
Like they all had quipped.

An aching had settled
Inside my skeleton,

A begging to be healed.

How can you become strong
And resilient, when death
Looks on, offering the
Solace that you desire.

Weakened from the beginning,
Longing for the quiet—
Welcoming with open arms.

No Instructions

Tell me where to put my anger.
My rage that boils, overheats
And runs over my high edges.

Can't find a place to store it
All and I don't want to slip.

Tell me what to do with the wrath
That makes me tremble and feel as
If my ribs are turned to blades.

Everything sharpened with fury.
Everything makes me bleed.

But perhaps the release is what I need.
My body is tired from clinging.

White knuckles weakened now,

As I try to grasp my anger.

Can't hold on much longer,

Tell me where to put my anger

So that I can finally rest.

Threadbare

Tear me apart, skin and bone,
Until you discover
Why I feel this way

Why am I not enough?
This sadness that lingers
I feel it in my hands,
The longing to create, to inspire

But my heart aches and
My knees hurt, the altar
I chose broken, abandoned,

Spirit hell bound for surely
Something is missing inside
As if the winter settled inside
My soul and never melted away.

Rip my flesh off, and inspect

My ligaments, what holds me
Together may surprise us both

For everything feels threadbare
And not enough, I am not enough,
I hand myself over to you
Maybe you can mend me

Stitch me back together,
Pull my grief out and gently
Leave a little happiness inside

I want to be enough.

Confessions

Gripping my bathroom sink,
The porcelain too strong to break
Beneath my bleeding palms.

No one has ever been more cruel
To me than I have been.

I have love inside me.
Somewhere, I know this
But it's not easy to find.

The maze of hate grows thicker and
Thicker—too many thorns
To pull apart and find my way.

I don't want to give in to rage
But I long to feel something.
Don't let me disappear, screaming.
My words fall flat on the face

In the mirror, for she'll never

Love me back.

Slowly Slipping

Hold me, arms wrapped
Tighter than a corset.

Even as I sleep, whisper
Words of affection.

Until that's all I know,
And all that will play
On repeat in my mind.

No longer myself
As I slowly
Forget
You

Until Death
Takes your place.

HOMESICK

Memories lost, scattered amongst
The dim stars in the inky sky above.

When I hear laughter,
Suddenly I'm homesick.

New wounds every time,
Unable to heal from before.

Rage hides beneath the surface,
For loneliness is a burden to bear.

When will the bleeding stop?
My heart continues to beat,

My love for you clings hopelessly
Despite the venom I let in.

SOMETHING BETTER

I have to become something better.

This anger rooted inside
Festers, grows, ruins me.

Every time your name
Is mentioned, wrath rules.
My heart is never enough.

Can I be your sunlight? Your echo,
As you murmur words of affection?

I must become something better
So that you can finally love me.

PART II:

WHAT IS LOVE?

RIPE STRAWBERRIES

By touch— skin as soft as the finest silks.
By smell— fresh cut lilies and roses,
Linger long after you're gone.

My love, with eyes whose sparkle
Rivals the starry sky, and lips
As tempting as ripe strawberries.
You are a dream embodied.

My love, a lifetime with you
Is simply not long enough.
You hold my heart in yours.

In Our Garden

Lay me in the garden,
Where I spent my days
Basking in the sunlight,
Reading by the trees.

The gentle breeze against
My skin, tinged with lilac.

The wind will whisper
All your words, your stories—
That you'll tell my grave.

Bury me in our garden
So that you can visit
Comfortably, until your grief is
No longer a burden to bear
But a translation of love.
Don't worry, the moon
will keep me company.

Fragrant Bouquet

Grabbing roses by their thorns,

The blood dripping down my palms—

A different kind of love letter

Lost amongst the beauty

That I hand to you.

My heart withers

Along with the flowers.

SEAMLESS

Weave us seamlessly together,
Like vines, smothering all the blossoming
Flowers, clawing their way towards the sun.

This manifestation of love—

An unholy phenomenon
They claim, yet I continue to stare
Directly on.

Captivate me until
We both return to the soil.

Find Me

When your thoughts are loud, who do you go to?
Do you seek the solace of the darkness,
The comfort the silence brings?

Are you safe there amongst the shadows,
Your heart wounded and bleeding?

Are your thoughts racing too fast,
Do you lay down in a field of stars?

Give me your heart to mend and
I'll weave it back together with a piece
Of mine, under the moonlight.

When your thoughts are loud

Find me in the darkness—

Where I'll hold your heart once more.

And lend you a shoulder as the

Universe looks away—for it too

Was made from many broken things.

Red Threads

Wrap your hand around mine once more.
Let the world around us melt away.

Intimacy beyond murmured
Declarations of love—soul mates.

Your fate so intricately woven with mine
Not even the sisters could cut us apart.

Find me in the stars after I'm gone.
I'll guide you home to me, don't worry.

BROKEN OATH

Am I just shadow and bone
Barely held together,
Everything just out of reach?

Confess my sins, my love.
For you, to the souls in the underworld.
Perhaps they'll find you first.

Am I just a broken oath
You spontaneously took?
I gave you my heart

And you cut me down like weeds,

Am I just a figment of your past,
Floating away, like the ferryman
Just a passing memory?

Past Relationships

Can you love a sinner

With a heart wrapped in greed
And lungs full of hollow promises?

Their eyes sparkle as they speak.
You're mesmerized even as you
Know you should leave.

Can you love someone
Who doesn't think about you
The moment you're gone?

You hang on to every word, every
Touch causes your heart to race.
You can love a sinner, but
They can't love you.
Yet, you still mourn the
Beginning as much as the end.

BOTTLED LOVE

Hints of fresh roses and vanilla

Linger, mixed with bergamot and

Time—an invitation, our

Clandestine relationship,

Clinging to your words.

Submerge me in your affection.

Such a resinous action, lock

Away my heart, stifled with cedar

And oak; carve our initials before

You leave, keep the key.

A piece of us forever

Remains with the other, as

We go our separate ways

MASKED

Made a mask of papier-mâché,
Hiding my frown from your view,
From you, yet the tears ruined it all.

It is okay not to love me.

Made a mask of porcelain
Hiding my scowl, but still there are cracks.
You took steps back, until I was alone,

Wanting nothing but to be loved.

How can you slip away so easily
When I hid it all? I molded myself
Into something I thought you wanted.

CUPID CAN BE CRUEL

The harsh words, tone discordant,
Filling my grave with each syllable.
Time running out on our moments
Together—painful yet how
Excruciatingly beautiful
It was to love you.

Forever stitched into my heart
Are my memories of your smile,
Your melodious laugh, with eyes
Closed, for fate dueled out.
I breathe in your perfume once
More, hoping it will linger
Long after you're gone,
In love with another.

DIFFICULT TO DEVOUR

Can you just whisper
That you love me?
Perhaps your words
Will echo inside and
Cause the walls to crack,
To disintegrate and
Crumble into pieces.

Please, for what is love
But ripened pomegranates?
Messy and difficult to devour
But beautiful and worth
The mess in the end.

CANDLE WAX

Each day I burn the
Candles you left behind,

Melted down to just the wick
In hopes to lure you back
To me—my mind can't handle
The silence without you.

I let the wax soften and
Disintegrate, hoping that
My feelings will follow.

Carving Our Initials

How do we know we're in love?
That we've found that soul that will
Easily mold into our own.

Rewire your heart—impossible
for heartache is a part of life
and, my love, we're all destined for pain.

But how can they know
This pain that won't stop?
Gasping for air, my lungs

Can't get enough, your touch
Like etchings left on tree barks.
Faded and weathered over time

But still there, nonetheless.
I can run my fingers over them
And know we existed together.

In another time, maybe I wouldn't

Have loved you as much to feel

This way without you around.

Moonflowers in Bloom

Emotions like white noise—
Always there, dimly present
But blocked like memories.

Then, as moonflowers bloom,
Take me to the night we met.

My love, so sweet the night,
Your soul comes alive under the stars.
Laughter, carried by the breeze.

I can feel your lips on mine,
Your touch lingers, imprinted
On my soul, forever a part of me.

It takes me to the night we met.

Every day without you, haunted
Of the past, the potential.

And as the moonflowers wilt,

So too, do I—my heart shriveling.

Forever broken, for I buried a

Piece with you long ago.

WIND WILL GRAZE

My memory loves you
Despite missing you more than
I can remember days with you.

Perhaps one day, when I lay
Flowers on your grave,
The wind will graze my skin.

And my heart will swell
And no tears will fall.

My memory loves you
And that feeling is something
I will take to my own grave.

POCKETS FULL OF ROCKS

There's a part of me that will always be 8 and
Showing you all the cool rocks that I found outside.
The eagerness and excitement nestled within
The memory of your smiling face.

There's a part of me that will always be 14 and
Finding her voice to describe art over coffee
With you in a museum; the brief moments of
Discussion cherished for years to come.

There's a part of me that will always be 18 and
Nervous about going to college states away.
Seeking comfort in your warm embrace before you
Drive away, you told me that you were proud.

There's a part of me that will always miss you.
No matter my age in real life, because
In my memories we sit side by side and
Spend our days talking about paintings.

And you ask me if I have any little rocks
In my pockets to show you, we laugh.

There's a part of you that I will
Always carry around with me.

COINS FOR TWO

Three years, ten months, or simply
Days remain—your time with me
Precious, memorable, lasting.

For when the sisters decide to cut
Your thread, I will join you my sweet.
For I cannot face a sunny day
Without your smile or a rainy night,
Without your laughter and warmth.

The beacon of my life, so when
Your light dims and fades away
I will I join you on the skiff,
Greeting Charon with coins ready.

Three years, ten months, or simply,
Days remain—I'll take any, and all,
Time with you, my sweet.

Envelops Me

I dreamt of your laughter

Filling every corner
Of the darkness
That envelops
Me each day.

It's welcoming,
I wrap myself
In the warmth
Of your memories.

Final Love Letter

Memories linger longer than our time together.
They glimmer in and out like fireflies.

Sometimes all it takes is a whiff of sunflowers
And you're standing next to me laughing.

Other times they roll in suddenly, like waves
Crashing onto my heart and we're holding
Hands as you gulp your final breaths.

But even as the tears fall, and the
Heartache returns, I'm never angry.
I'd never let the bitterness tinge my memories.

Grief is like a final love letter
Left unopened, yellowing with age.

For any time spent with you, or
Just remembering you, is a gift.

WANDERING

Once my shadow, attached
To me; clinging as we both
Wandered through life.

Now just a dream of mine—
You're hazy and trapped
Wandering in the past.

MOURNING SKY

Memories slipping,
Slipping,
Slip.

Confusion, frustration—
My hazel stare.

Time passes like the night sky
Gentle and quiet, then darkness.
Envelops us, mourning doesn't start
When you die, but when you're gone.

Your vacant eyes
Glimmer—recognition.

Slip,
Slipping,
Memories have slipped.

IF HE'D LET ME

I would count the stars twice
If you asked me to.

I would swim across oceans
If you needed me to.

I would take your place in Death
If he'd let me go for you.

Yet here I am, on a cliff below.
The stars, the salty air fills my lungs
As I scream for your return.

PROMISED THE SUN

The first time I died was when you left.

Perhaps the second time I die,
When Death takes my hand and leads me
On to the other side; perhaps the stars
Will shine brighter that night as I join you.

You promised that you would give me the sun
And when you left, I was given the moon—
The darkness, too silent and lonely.
I sought Death with a hunger he feared.

The warmth of you vanished from my days.

HAUNT ME

Come back to me, my sweet,
As whispers under the moonlight,
Or in my dreams, the ache
Becoming too much to bear.

Come back to me, my sweet,
You took my heart when you left.
Haunt me, if it means just once
More we can be together.

Come back to me, my sweet,
Before I succumb to my grief.
Gasping for air between sobs.

Perhaps Death needs company.

PART III :

CONFESSING TO DEATH

TRACE OF ME

I don't know the version of *me*
That lives inside your head
But it's not the *me* that I am today.

I don't know what age I am
Inside your memories,
Or if you remember me at all.

But the last time we spoke,
There was an intensity in your stare—
Your eyes focused on my face,

Confusion lurking behind the haze.
And as my name left your tongue,
I knew this visit would be etched
Forever in my recollection of you.

I will remember you
long after you've forgotten

Any trace of me.

FERRY MY MEMORIES

After death, even if I cannot
Carry your memories with me
Across the River Styx,
I will know that the ache
Is caused by a bond so strong that

I made Death think twice.

For recounting my feelings
And everything missing
Will surely bore Hades.

Maybe he'll let me keep you
At the back of my mind.

Home For Two

Built a home for my memories
In the grief you left behind.

And sometimes, I'm homesick
For this place with no map.

For you live there forever
And I stumble upon you there.

In a home I've built—it's shaky
But permanent, I'll find you
There after the funeral.

DEARLY DEPARTED

Grief molded to my ribcage
Every breath tinged with goodbye.

My lungs full of every
Word I never said,
until I'm overwhelmed.

Screaming at your name
Freshly carved in stone,

The other headstones
Are my only witnesses.

Ghosts in the Daylight

You're a shell
of who you once were—

A hollow smile,
With eyes that see
Those that aren't there.

Your mind,
no longer the same.

The love remains, for to me,
You'll always hover
Behind my closed eyes.

Forever carried with me—
A collage of memories,

Not just the last.

PLEASE STAY

The last time we were together
You smiled like nothing was wrong.
And we talked about mundane things
Over coffee, but you forgot bits and
Pieces, needing help unlike before.

Once a pillar of strength and independence,
The one I sought for guidance.
Now fragile and fading.

Unknown to me, it'd be our last
Normal conversation.
Grief is a funny feeling—for while
You're still alive, you're gone.

Vintage Furs

Every milestone is brought on
By a quiet cry on my closet floor,
Surrounded by your vintage fur coats.

The scent of mothballs covers
Any trace of how they used
To smell like your home.

Glimpses of you, memories
Surround me still, as if you're
In the kitchen cooking away,

Listening to every word I have
To say to this empty closet.

Visit Once More

I don't want to drown
In this flood of memories
On a random Tuesday.

Days, months, and even years later,

You never understood
The impact you made on me.

But drowning is a quiet,
Desperate reprieve and maybe
It's the only way
To visit you once more.

GRIEF, I AM

I am the shadows
That lurk into your soul,
That tug at your feelings,
Unraveling your strength—
All those walls you built,
All those safeguards you hold.

I am the tears
That fall as your chest convulses.
Your body trembles and you're
Unable to keep your composure.
All your feelings bubble up,
All your memories creep in.

You can push me down,

You can pretend I'm not here

But I'll always be there.

Beneath the surface and

Intertwined in your being

Every fiber poisoned by me.

Reunited in Death

I'll carry my loss
On my tongue.
Find me crying to death,

Gasping for air;
Waiting, longing
For quiet.

How can you live
Without
Your favorite
Person?

A cruel lesson
In life I refuse
To learn.

Waiting, longing
To be reunited.

I USED TO BE

I'm inside out, memories blur.
Anger fills my veins
Then just as suddenly grief
Crashed into me, my mind
Is no longer my own.

A ghost of myself lingers
Just out of reach.
She always frowns.

For I'll never be
My old self–*don't*
let me be gone–I cry,
I plead, but she's
Simply a passenger
On my way to death.

STAINED GLASS SCARS

Why is it that stained glass is breathtakingly
Beautiful, but when I cut myself and bleed
The stained remnants are never enough?

I know you by the state of your wrists.

Delicate scars decorate your body—
A map of despair and grief
Like vines they suffocate, never enough.

I know you by the state of your eyes.

Haunted by the past, with a tinge of sadness
The storm's grey gaze lingers, then you look away.
Silence stretches over us, time passes.

I stare in the mirror again, I know you.

SEASIDE

Waves crescendo, crashing

Into me, pulling me

Further and further

Into the darkness.

The inky water filling

My lungs and enveloping

My entire being – inside

and out – until

I succumb to the sea.

DOES ANYTHING CHANGE?

I don't believe in God anymore.
For years, every week I went
To their house of worship and prayed.
I mumbled along and sang the songs,
Letting the sermon wash over me.

I loved the way the light trickled
In through the stained glass windows—
A kaleidoscope of colors
Dancing on the perish attendance.

But despite the hours spent there,
Nothing has ever changed for me.

Death remains my closest confidante.

STAINED CHAISE

Opened up my scars—
I apologize for the blood
Stains, but not much else.

Letting the past ooze
Out, the memories glimmer;
Good and bad, accuracy hazy.

Mind woozy as my veins
Slowly empty on the antique
Velvet chaise—my final rest.

Lids heavy, head rolls back.
The baroque crown molding is
Calming and Death's hand
On my shoulder, welcomed now.

After Death

When I pass, will you linger?

A moment or two longer, each
Time you visit my grave
Until one day you weep
Falling to your knees, hands
Clenching fists of dirt.
Will you scream until you're hoarse?

The pain unbearable,
The memories, unforgettable.

When I pass, will you survive?

FLUENT IN SILENCE

Aimlessly wandering through
The limbo I created for myself,
No audience to perform for.

Drowning in sorrow is a quiet action.

Unmasked, with grief for company.
No regrets linger, it's something else—
I've been haunting my daydreams.

No one notices the façade, they speak
But I'm only fluent in silence.

Commit me to Death's door.
I've decided to knock politely.

DEATH IS A TEASE

The darkness stale, heavy
Is the feeling on my chest.
As if a body pins me down
But I've been here before.

Before I open my eyes,
My heart is pounding, the echo
Louder than thunder in the sky.

Once again, he's lurking in
The shadows—Death is a tease.

The only way to know
You're alive is to dream.

How many times will he stop by?
A lurking presence, quiet but known.
The marble beneath me is cold.
The air now damp, my eyes flitter,

In a coffin now—no, a mausoleum!

But he's there, his hands gripping
The edge of my stone casket,
Closer now than ever before.

No face beneath the hood,
No heart or soul within.
Panic seeps in as my body shakes.

Time is never the same when
You're asleep, it lasts forever.

It's just a nightmare, a reverie
For the dead—but I'm alive.
To dream is to be alive,
I murmur over and over and over.

About The Author

Brianna Malotke is a writer based in the Pacific Northwest. She's an active member of the Horror Writers Association and was the co-chair of the Seattle Chapter (2023-2025). Malotke has over 90 publications in various magazines, zines, and anthologies. While most of her work is within the realms of horror and nightmares, she loves writing about love and relationships.

Her standalone poetry collections include *Don't Cry on Cashmere*, *Fashion Trends*, *Deadly Ends*, and *Lost Cherry*. In the fall of 2023 she was a "Writer in Residence" at the Chateau d'Orquevaux in France and she's been daydreaming about the next time she can get lost in the French countryside ever since.

www.malotkewrites.com

www.ingramcontent.com/pod-product-compliance
Lightning Source LLC
Chambersburg PA
CBHW050448150626
46551CB00029B/2153